W9-CBX-630

CAREERS IN THE
BUILDING TRADES

A GROWING DEMAND

Masonry Worker

Careers in the Building Trades
A Growing Demand

Apprenticeships

Carpenter

Construction & Building Inspector

Electrician

Flooring Installer

Heating and Cooling Technician

Masonry Worker

Plumber

Roofer

Working in Green Construction

CAREERS IN THE
BUILDING TRADES
A GROWING DEMAND

Masonry Worker

Andrew Morkes

MASON CREST

Mason Crest
450 Parkway Drive, Suite D
Broomall, Pennsylvania 19008
(866) MCP-BOOK (toll-free)
www.masoncrest.com

First printing

9 8 7 6 5 4 3 2 1
ISBN (hardback) 978-1-4222-4117-2

ISBN (series) 978-1-4222-4110-3

ISBN (ebook) 978-1-4222-7687-7

Cataloging-in-Publication Data on file with the Library of Congress

NATIONAL
HIGHLIGHTS

Developed and Produced by National Highlights Inc.
Proofreader: Mika Jin
Interior and cover design: Yolanda Van Cooten
Production: Michelle Luke

CONTENTS

KEY ICONS TO LOOK FOR:

Words to understand: These words with their easy-to-understand definitions will increase the reader's understanding of the text while building vocabulary skills.

Sidebars: This boxed material within the main text allows readers to build knowledge, gain insights, explore possibilities, and broaden their perspectives by weaving together additional information to provide realistic and holistic perspectives.

Educational Videos: Readers can view videos by scanning our QR codes, providing them with additional educational content to supplement the text. Examples include news coverage, moments in history, speeches, iconic sports moments and much more!

Text-dependent questions: These questions send the reader back to the text for more careful attention to the evidence presented there.

Research projects: Readers are pointed toward areas of further inquiry connected to each chapter. Suggestions are provided for projects that encourage deeper research and analysis.

Series glossary of key terms: This back-of-the-book glossary contains terminology used throughout this series. Words found here increase the reader's ability to read and comprehend higher-level books and articles in this field.

INTRODUCTION

The Trades: Great Careers, Good Money, and Other Rewards

Trades workers play a major role in the success of economies throughout the world. They keep the power on (electricians), use bricks and natural and human-made stone to build walls and other masonry structures (masonry workers), and install and repair pipes that carry water, fuel, and other liquids to, from, and within businesses, factories, and homes (plumbers and pipefitters), among many other job duties. Yet despite their pivotal role in our society, only 6 percent of students consider a career in the trades, according to ExploretheTrades. org. Why? Because many young people have misconceptions about the trades. They have been told that the trades are low-paying, lack job security, and other untruths. In fact, working in the trades is one of the best career choices you can make. The following paragraphs provide more information on why a career in the trades is a good idea.

Good pay. Contrary to public perception, skilled trades workers earn salaries that place them firmly in the middle class. For example, average annual salaries for brickmasons in the United States are $53,440, according to the U.S. Department of Labor. This salary is higher than the average earnings for some careers that require a bachelor's or graduate degree—including meeting planners ($52,020), social workers ($50,710), counselors ($49,740), and recreational therapists ($48,190). Trades workers who become managers or who launch their own businesses can have earnings that range from $90,000 to $200,000.

Strong employment prospects. There are shortages of trades workers throughout the world, according to the human resource consulting firm ManpowerGroup. In fact, trades workers are the most in-demand occupational field in the Americas, Europe,

the Middle East, and Africa. They ranked fourth in the Asia-Pacific region. Stonemasons are in especially strong demand in Germany, Switzerland, Sweden, and Australia, according to the recruitment firm Michael Page. Employment for masonry workers in the United States is expected to grow faster than the average for all careers during the next decade.

Provides a comfortable life without a bachelor's or graduate degree. For decades in the United States and other countries, there has been an emphasis on earning a college degree as the key to life success. But studies show that only 35 percent of future jobs in the United States will require a four-year degree or higher. With college tuition continuing to increase and the chances of landing a good job out of college decreasing, a growing number of people are entering apprenticeship programs to prepare for careers in the trades. And unlike college students, apprentices receive a salary while learning and they don't have to pay off loans after they complete their education. It's a good feeling to start your career without $50,000 to $200,000 in college loans.

Rewarding work environment and many career options. A career in the trades is fulfilling because you get to use both your hands and your head to solve problems and make the world a better place. Masonry workers work at homes, commercial building construction sites, in historical restoration, or in other places where stonework needs to be built or repaired. Many trades workers launch their own businesses.

Jobs can't be offshored. Trades careers involve hands-on work that requires the worker to be on-site to do his or her job. As a result, there is no chance that your position will be offshored to a foreign country. In an uncertain employment atmosphere, that's encouraging news.

7

Job opportunities are available throughout the United States and the world. There is a need for trades workers in small towns and big cities. If demand for their skills is not strong in their geographic area, they can move to other cities, states, or countries where demand is higher.

Are the Trades Right for Me?

Test your interest in the trades. How many of these statements do you agree with?

☐ **My favorite class in school is shop.**

☐ **I like to build and repair things.**

☐ **I like doing household repairs.**

☐ **I like to use power and hand tools.**

☐ **I like projects that allow me to work with my hands and use my creativity.**

☐ **I enjoy observing work at construction sites.**

☐ **I like to watch home-repair shows on TV and the internet.**

☐ **I don't mind getting dirty when I work on a project.**

☐ **I am good at math.**

If many of the statements above describe you, then you should consider a career in the trades. But you don't need to select a career right now. Check out this book on a career as a masonry worker and other books in the series to learn more about occupational paths in the trades. Good luck with your career exploration!

8

■ *The Taj Mahal in Agra, India*

Words to Understand

Great Wall of China: A series of walls and fortifications in China that stretch approximately 13,170 miles (21,196 kilometers), although portions are gone or are in ruins. It was first constructed 2,700 years ago, and it is a top tourist destination and one of the greatest wonders of the world.

historical landmarks: Buildings or other structures that are protected under law because they have special value because of historical, cultural, or other factors.

self-employed: Working for oneself as a small business owner, rather than for a corporation or other employer. Self-employed people must generate their own income, and they must provide their own fringe benefits (such as health insurance).

Taj Mahal: An immense and beautiful mausoleum (tomb) in India that was constructed out of white marble between 1631 and 1648 A.D. by order of the Mughal emperor Shah Jahan in memory of his favorite wife, Mumtaz Maha.

CHAPTER 1

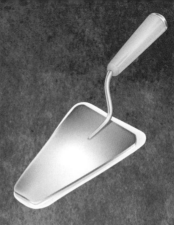

What Do Masonry Workers Do?

What do the Great Wall of China, the Taj Mahal, and your school likely have in common? They were all built by masonry workers. Masonry is an ancient trade. Its origins have been traced back about 6,000 years. *Masonry workers*, who are sometimes known as *masons*, use brick, tile, cement, stone (marble, granite, limestone, etc.), and other materials to create surfaces and structures such as buildings, walls, fences, fireplaces, bridges, roads, sidewalks, chimneys and high-temperature furnaces, and other structures. Still others focus on repairing and conserving masonry in historical landmarks or other structures. Masons work for construction companies, small contractors, and government agencies. Others operate their own businesses.

Many aspiring masons prepare for the field by completing an apprenticeship. Others participate in training programs at technical schools or learn via on-the-job training. The U.S. military and other militaries also provide training in cement masonry and concrete finishing. Many cities, states, and countries require masonry contractors to be licensed. Some masonry workers earn certification credentials to show customers that they have met the highest standards established by their industry.

■ *Well-known actress and comedienne Whoopi Goldberg once worked as a bricklayer.*

11

They Were Masonry Workers!?

Actress and comedienne Whoopi Goldberg has played a nun (*Sister Act*), psychic (*Ghost*), and many other popular film roles, but did you know that before achieving cinematic fame, she was a bricklayer? As a fledgling actress, she worked as a bricklayer and in other jobs to pay the bills. Here are a few other well-known people who worked as bricklayers:

- **Arnold Schwarzenegger**, the famous bodybuilder, actor, and former governor of California, started his own bricklaying business with a bodybuilder friend to make ends meet before he hit the big time.

- Before actor **Sean Connery** became the swashbuckling spy James Bond in the popular British film series, he worked as a bricklayer to support himself.

- The famed British leader **Winston Churchill** was an amateur bricklayer. He built the walls of a garden at one of his homes, as well as a cottage for one of his daughters.

A career as a mason can be physically demanding, but it's also interesting and rewarding. A well-constructed brick home or other structure can last hundreds of years. There are not many careers in which the worker can walk down the street and say, "I built that!" Masonry is one of them.

■ *Check out the top ten reasons to become a bricklayer:*

12

■ *There is strong demand for bricklayers in many countries.*

Bricklayers

Brick is made from clay or shale and fired in a kiln at about 2,000 degrees Fahrenheit (1,093 degrees Celsius) to make the materials firm and bind together. It has been used for thousands of years to construct buildings, bridges, and other structures because it is durable; fire-resistant; and comes in many sizes, colors, and textures.

Bricklayers build and repair walls, fireplaces, chimneys, floors, and other structures with brick, terra cotta, concrete or glass block, precast masonry panels, and other masonry materials. They are sometimes called *brickmasons* and *blockmasons*. They perform many duties, including:

- Reading and working from blueprints and other plans to calculate the types and amounts of materials to use

- Erecting scaffolding and ladders to prepare for the work

- Excavating (digging out) foundations, building a wood frame, and mixing and pouring the concrete to build a foundation (strong base) in preparation for building the main structure

How to Build a Small Garden Wall

Here are the basic steps a bricklayer would take to build a small garden wall. The process is more complicated than can be explained in a book, but reviewing these steps will you give a general idea of what a bricklayer does to complete a simple home project.

1. Measure and mark off the work area where the wall is to be built.

2. Remove dirt from the work area to a depth of about six inches (15.24 centimeters).

3. Use wood to build a frame that will hold the concrete for the foundation. Set up the wood frame.

4. Mix and pour the concrete into the foundation. Let the concrete dry.

5. Measure and mark the center of the wall with a measuring tape and chalk line.

6. Apply mortar to the area where the first row of bricks will be placed.

7. Mix mortar and place it on the trowel (this is called "buttering").

8. Use the trowel to apply the mortar to the brick, and then place the brick carefully in the row.

9. Remove excess mortar from the brick and work area, and repeat the process, using a level or mason's line to ensure that the bricks are aligned correctly. Finish the row.

10. Use the trowel to apply mortar to the top of the first row. Start the next row with a half-size brick so that the second-row layout is staggered; this will make the wall stronger. Use a brick chisel and hammer to cut the brick. Use the trowel to apply mortar to the short edge of the brick that will connect to the adjoining brick. Continue to use the level and mason's line as the wall is built to ensure that it is straight, and the bricks are aligned correctly.

11. Fill any holes in the seams with mortar.

12. Allow the mortar to dry and the bricks to set.

13. Strike/point the dried mortar between the bricks to give the brickwork a professional finish.

14. Brush the brickwork with a soft hand brush to remove any excess mortar from the brickwork face.

- Sealing foundations with water-resistant materials
- Applying mortar to building surfaces and bricks; placing bricks in rows, designs, or shapes; and spreading mortar between joints
- Cutting and trimming brick to the necessary size by using hand tools or by operating a brick cutting machine
- Repairing and maintaining bricks, cement blocks, and other masonry units

Some bricklayers specialize. *Pointing, cleaning, and caulking workers* repair mortar and brickwork that has become damaged. They caulk and weatherproof masonry, as needed. They use an angle grinder, tuck pointer, and other tools to tuckpoint (clean out and remortar) cracked and crumbling masonry. (In some settings, a general mason handles all the pointing, cleaning, caulking, and tuckpointing tasks.) *Refractory masons* work in industrial settings. They specialize in installing firebrick, gunite (a mixture of cement, water, and sand that is applied through a pressure hose to produce a thick, hard layer of concrete used to build tunnels and for other purposes), and refractory tile, which retains its strength in high-temperature boilers, furnaces, cupolas (a cylindrical furnace for refining metals), and soaking pits.

■ *A mason mixes concrete.*

Concrete Masons and Finishers

Concrete is a common construction material that is made of sand, conglomerate gravel, pebbles, broken stone, or slag (stony waste) in a mortar or cement mix. The ancient Romans made concrete by mixing volcanic rock and lime (a calcium-containing inorganic mineral) to form a mortar. Concrete was used to build the Roman Pantheon (a well-preserved temple that was built between A.D. 118 and 125) and many other structures. Concrete masonry units—which are also known as cement blocks, concrete blocks, and foundation blocks—have been used since the 1870s in building construction. Today, concrete is the most widely-used construction material (by tonnage) on earth.

Concrete masons place concrete masonry units in rows to build the structural frame of a building or its individual components. They may also mix and pour concrete to create sidewalks, floors, ceilings, beams, and columns. They smooth and finish the concrete, apply surface treatments or curing (hardening) treatments, and may color concrete surfaces to make them look more attractive or to match the color of existing concrete. They are experts regarding the effects of weather conditions (humidity, heat, cold, etc.) on the curing of the concrete.

Stonemasons

Stonemasons use their hands, special hammers, diamond-blade saws, and other tools to build stone walls, as well as stone floors, window frames, archways, and ornamental (decorative) garden pieces. They use both natural-cut stone, such as granite and marble, and artificial stone, which is made from concrete, marble chips, or other masonry materials. Some stonemasons repair damaged stonework or memorial headstones.

Terrazzo Masons

Terrazzo consists of chips of marble, glass, or other aggregates (a combination of several elements) that are placed in colored cement, then ground smooth and polished to a beautiful shine. Terrazzo was accidentally discovered by mosaic artisans in the fifteenth century. After working on flooring indoors, they swept the marble debris out onto their terraces, known as terrazzi. As the debris smoothed due to foot traffic, the artisans realized the beauty of this effect. Terrazzo became very popular. Michelangelo used terrazzo in St. Peter's Basilica in what is now Vatican City (an enclave in Rome, Italy).

■ *Terrazzo workers often create beautiful designs, such as this fish pattern, with stone.*

Terrazzo masons, who are also known as *terrazzo workers* and *finishers,* create decorative terrazzo floors, patios, and other structures. Much of their set-up work (pouring, leveling, and finishing concrete) is similar to what cement masons do. Once the concrete or other building material (epoxy, resin) has been poured or applied, terrazzo workers create decorative finishes by creatively placing fine marble chips into concrete or other material. Once the terrazzo sets, masons fix any depressions or imperfections with a grinder or hand tools to create a smooth and attractive finish.

Work Environments

A large amount of masonry work is done outdoors, so expect to work in a wide range of weather conditions. Masons do not work in the rain because water is the enemy of a well-constructed masonry structure. In this situation, they may work under a protective covering. Masons also work indoors to install floors, interior walls, decorative elements, and other structures. Some newly constructed buildings may not yet have heat, so masons need to dress warmly in these instances.

Work schedules vary for masons, but most work forty hours a week, Monday through Friday—although longer hours (including weekends) may be necessary when a project is on deadline or if a project has been started later in the day and needs to be finished before the mortar or concrete sets. Additionally, more work is typically available in the warmer months, which may require masons to work more hours during these seasons and fewer in cold seasons.

17

Construction sites are often muddy, dirty, loud, and dangerous. Masons wear protective gloves, hard hats, dust masks, safety goggles (when cutting stone), and other safety gear to protect themselves. Travel to various job sites is required, so you'll need a driver's license and a trustworthy vehicle.

■ *Learn more about a career as a union cement mason:*

Becoming a Boss

Masons who have a minimum of five years of experience can be promoted to the position of *foreman*. In this career, you'll oversee a team of masonry workers as they mix, pour, and finish concrete; build walls or arches; create terrazzo flooring; and perform other tasks. Major job responsibilities for foremen include:

- Keeping crews on schedule
- Occasionally pitching in to help if a job is on a tight deadline or if there is a shortage of masons on site
- Meeting with construction managers during the project to make sure that the work is being completed on-time, on-budget, and meeting other project guidelines
- Ordering building materials and ensuring that all equipment is in good working order
- Ensuring that masons follow safety rules and that the worksite does not have any safety issues that could cause injury to workers
- Checking finished work to ensure that it meets building codes and project specifications

- Evaluating the work of apprentices to ensure that their skills and masonry knowledge are improving
- Traveling to multiple construction sites to manage work teams.

Starting Your Own Contracting Business

Are you comfortable managing others? Do you enjoy making your own decisions? Does the idea of building your own business from the ground up sound exciting? If so, a career as a *masonry contractor* is a good choice. A masonry contractor is simply a skilled mason who owns his or her business. Owning your own contracting firm is a popular career path for some types of masons. In fact, 30 percent of bricklayers in the United States are self-employed, according to the U.S. Department of Labor. That's much higher than the average (10.1 percent) for people in all careers. On the other hand, only about 2.4 percent of terrazzo workers are self-employed.

The Pros and Cons of Being a Masonry Contractor

Pros

- You get to be your own boss.
- You can create your own work schedule (e.g., work extra one day, so you can take the next day off to go to a ball game or extend your weekend).
- You have the chance to receive much higher earnings than a salaried mason if your business is successful.

Cons

- It can be stressful to keep your business running smoothly.
- You'll be responsible for advertising your business, preparing estimates, scheduling appointments, and managing staff.
- Contractors typically work much longer hours—especially when launching their businesses—than salaried masons do.

Related Career Paths

Masons who complete additional education and training are qualified to work in many related fields. Here are a few popular options:

Construction inspectors examine buildings and other structures to ensure that they have been built correctly. *Building inspectors* examine homes, condominiums, townhomes, and other new or previously owned buildings. They are also known as *home inspectors*. Some inspectors specialize in examining the condition of structural masonry. Many inspectors have earned a certificate or an associate degree that includes courses in building inspection, construction technology, and home inspection. Some also receive certification from the Masonry Institute of America.

Framing carpenters measure, cut, and assemble wood and other materials to create the basic framework for floor, wall, and roof framing, window installation, and exterior door installation. They are also known as *rough carpenters*. Carpenters train for the field by completing an apprenticeship or on-the-job training, earning a certificate or associate degree from a community or technical college, or receiving training in the military.

Cost estimators are experts in one or more construction specialties (masonry, electrical, etc.). They create estimates of how much money, time, materials, and labor will be required to complete a construction project or create a product. Cost estimators who work in the construction industry typically need a bachelor's degree in construction management, engineering, or a related field.

Plasterers apply plaster to ceilings, interior walls, and other areas of buildings, as well as to wire, wood, or metal. Plasterers prepare for the field via an apprenticeship or on-the-job training.

Sculptors use hand and power tools, and their own creativity, to create three-dimensional works of art. They work with stone, wood, plaster, clay, and other materials. Many sculptors are self-taught, while others develop their skills by attending art colleges.

Staying Safe on the Job

Masonry workers are injured on the job at a higher average than all workers, according to the U.S. Department of Labor. The most common injuries include:

■ *Some masonry workers use their creative talents to create sculptures and other artistic works.*

- Cuts from sharp tools (chisels, trowels, etc.), sharp objects on the ground, or from accidents that occur while performing other tasks
- Musculoskeletal injuries caused by lifting heavy loads of bricks and other construction materials
- Broken bones, concussions, spinal cord injuries, and other injuries caused by falls from roofs, ladders, or scaffolds
- Heatstroke, heat exhaustion, and dehydration from work in extremely hot temperatures
- Serious sunburn
- Frostbite and hypothermia from working in extremely cold conditions
- Back injuries and muscle stress/strains
- Eye injuries caused by falling or swinging objects

■ *Masons frequently work outdoors and at heights.*

- Tendonitis, carpel tunnel syndrome, and pinched nerves caused by repetitive motions
- Respiratory issues due to exposure to hazardous chemicals and fumes, and other toxic or carcinogenic substances such as silica dust
- Knee, leg, or other injuries caused by kneeling for long periods or slipping on wet or icy surfaces
- Hearing damage caused by loud noise from cutting/sawing materials

How to Stay Safe on the Job

Masons wear safety glasses, knee pads, dust masks or respirators, heavy gloves, earplugs, hardhats, and protective clothing to prevent injury. There are also many things they can do on-site to protect themselves, including:

- Start each work day by inspecting their worksite for safety issues (tripping or slipping hazards, sharp objects, frayed electrical cords, etc.) and fix the issues.
- Use a ladderlift, a human-, electrical-, or battery-powered device that transports heavy building materials (such as brick) up a ladder to a roof or other high area.
- Take regular breaks to reduce the chance of repetitive motion injuries.
- Alternate work tasks between hands to prevent or reduce fatigue and pain.
- Stay focused on the job to avoid cuts, bumps and bruises, and other injuries.
- Use a respirator, an artificial breathing device that will protect them from breathing in dust or other toxic substances such as silica.
- Use height-adjustable mortarboards to reduce forward bending.
- Use ladder tie-offs, straps that secure ladders to a roof or structure.

 Text-Dependent Questions

1. What do cement masons do?

2. What are some challenging aspects of a career as a masonry contractor?

3. What kinds of safety gear do masons use to protect themselves on the job?

 Research Project

Experiment by building a short wall that is made from brick, concrete blocks, or stones. Ask your shop teacher or a parent for help.

23

CHAPTER 2

Tools of the Trade

Cutting, Pounding, and Finishing Tools

blocking chisel: A heavy, wide chisel that is used when many blocks or bricks need to be split, and very clean cuts are needed. A blocking chisel is used in tandem with a mashing hammer, sledge hammer, or mallet.

brush: A hand tool that is used to remove powder residue, mortar stains, and other debris from stone work.

chisel: A hand tool with a shaped, sharp cutting edge that is used to cut, chip, or carve stone, wood, or metal. In masonry, chisels are used to shape, rough out, and split stone.

gauging trowel: A flat-bladed hand tool with a distinct rounded nose that is useful for finishing large joints and general mortar patching. It is usually about seven inches (17.78 centimeters) long.

mashing hammer: A type of hammer that is used in tandem with a chisel to split stone.

mason's hammer: A hand tool with one side that is square and flat (like a traditional hammer), and one that is sharp, like a small chisel.

mason's trowel: A point-nosed, flat-bladed hand tool—which is typically ten to eleven inches (25.4 to 27.94 centimeters) long—that is used to pick up and spread mortar. The shape of the blade allows the mason to apply the mortar in a very precise way. Also known as a *brick trowel*.

pointing trowel: This flat-bladed hand tool has a triangular tip that is used for pointing work. It is about six inches (15.24 centimeters) long.

power saw: A saw that is used to cut large quantities of block or brick. It is available in both a hand-held or table-mounted model.

powered mortar mixer: A machine that mixes large amounts of mortar.

tuck pointer: A finishing tool that is used to smooth the mortar-filled joints between bricks.

Safety Equipment

dust mask: A protective covering worn over the mouth and nose to reduce the inhalation of harmful substances when the mason is grinding or saw-cutting stone.

rubber gloves: Protective gloves worn by masons when they are wet-cutting masonry units onsite; the gloves protect against electric shock.

safety glasses: Protective gear that shields the eyes of masons from injury by pieces of stone chipped off during their work and other hazards.

Measuring/Guiding Tools

chalk line: A marking tool that is used by masons to snap chalk lines to get the alignment correct as they lay out a block wall on a concrete foundation.

level: A device that is used to establish a horizontal plane. It is comprised of a small glass tube that contains alcohol or a similar liquid and an air bubble.

mason's line: A nylon or polyester line that masons stretch between two corners (and anchor using flat-bladed steel pins) of a wall they are building. It allows them to work faster than if they had to constantly use a level to check their work, and the line helps them avoid bulges or hollows in the wall.

steel square: Used to make sure that corners are at a ninety-degree angle (if the mason is building a square or rectangular wall) during the construction process.

Computer Technology

building information modeling software: A computer application that uses a 3D model-based process that helps construction, architecture, and engineering professionals to more efficiently plan, design, build, and manage buildings and infrastructure.

office and customer management software: A computer application that helps users track finances and manage billing, draft correspondence, and perform other tasks.

CHAPTER 3

Terms of the Trade

bleeding: A negative development in which stone is stained by corrosive metals, oil-based putties, caulking, sealing compounds, minerals in the stone, or other compounds.

brick: A solid or partly hollow rectangular block of clay that has been baked in a kiln (oven) or by the sun until it is hard. Bricks are frequently used to construct walls and other structures, as well as for paving material.

building codes: A series of rules established by local, state, regional, and national governments that ensure safe construction.

buttering: The process of placing mortar on a masonry unit with a trowel.

cement: The binding element in both mortar and concrete, which is most frequently made of limestone, clay, silica sand, shells, and other materials. The most commonly-used type of cement is Portland cement. It is manufactured from limestone and clay. It is further categorized as a hydraulic cement because it hardens when combined with water.

chimney: A vertical fireproof structure that it is attached to a home or other building to provide draft for fireplaces and to send gaseous products of combustion to the outside air from fireplaces, boilers, or furnaces. It is commonly constructed out of brick or other types of stone.

concrete: A common construction material that is made of sand, conglomerate gravel, pebbles, broken stone, or slag in a mortar or cement matrix.

dowel: A cylindrical piece of steel that is used to hold stone in place.

dry wall: In the masonry sector, a stone wall that is built one stone on the other without mortar. This building style is generally used to construct retaining walls.

face: The exposed surface of a wall or masonry unit.

foundation: In a construction project, the part of the structure that connects it to the ground and evenly distributes the weight of the structure.

furrowing: The process of using a trowel to cut a small indent into the mortar bed to ready the mortar bed for the brick.

grout: A mixture of Portland cement and sand that is used to fill the seams between masonry units.

joint: The space between masonry units.

load-bearing wall: A wall that is typically constructed of sturdy materials (such as brick, concrete, or block) that serves as a support for other components of the structure. Also called a **bearing wall.**

masonry: Construction using durable materials such as tile, brick, cement, stone (marble, granite, limestone, etc.), or similar materials.

masonry units: An individual brick or block in masonry construction.

mortar: A mixture of cement, sand, lime, and water that is used to link masonry units.

mortarboard: A flat surface where mortar is readied for application. May also be called a **mudboard** or **hawk.**

mortar patching: The process of replacing cracked, missing, or otherwise damaged mortar with new mortar.

non-load-bearing wall: A wall that does not provide significant support for any components above it. Also called a **curtain wall.**

pitch: In construction, the angle of rise in degrees from a horizontal starting point.

plumb: A condition of being exactly vertical; measured with a plumb line.

proud: Slang for when one building component protrudes above another.

rebar: Steel bars that are added and embedded in masonry to increase its strength. Also known as **reinforcing bars**.

scaffold: A temporary raised structure that masonry workers, roofers, and other trades workers use to work at heights that would otherwise be hard to reach.

splitting block or brick: The process of using a mason's hammer (a hand tool that has one side that is square and flat, and one that is sharp, like a small chisel) to break stone. The chisel-like side is used to create a cutting line where the stone is to be split. The mason then gives the chisel a sharp hit with the traditional hammer side to get a clean break until the targeted stone is removed.

tooths: Projecting masonry units.

tuckpointing: The process of repairing mortar joints in brick or stone masonry walls. The old mortar is ground down or raked out to a certain depth, and then filled with new mortar.

weep hole: An opening placed in mortar joints of facing material that allows moisture to escape (rather than remain and cause damage to the stone).

wet-cutting: A process in which stone is cut with a saw that is equipped with a water hose that sprays water on the blade as the cut is made to reduce the creation of high levels of crystalline silica (tiny specks of concrete, sandstone, granite, and brick that can cause serious health problems if inhaled). Wet-cutting also helps equipment to last longer since the water reduces the amount of heat and dust generated by the cutting process—therefore reducing wear and tear.

■ *It's a good idea to take chemistry in high school to learn more about the chemical properties of stone and other substances.*

Words to Understand

apprenticeship: A formal training program that combines classroom instruction and supervised practical experience. Apprentices are paid a salary that increases as they obtain experience.

certificate: A credential that shows that a person has completed specialized education, passed a test, and met other requirements to qualify for work in a career or industry. They are offered by trade associations and colleges and universities. College certificate programs typically last six months to a year.

internship: A paid or unpaid learning opportunity in which a student works at a company or other employer to obtain experience. Internships can last anywhere from a few weeks to a year.

pension: A regular payment made to a retired person from a fund that the person and/or their employer has contributed to during the time they worked at the employer.

CHAPTER 4

Preparing for the Field and Making a Living

Educational Paths

If building and repairing walls, bridges, and other stone structures seems like a rock-solid career choice, your next step is to explore training opportunities. There are several educational paths from which to choose: participation in an apprenticeship (the most popular entry method), attending a technical school or community college, learning through informal methods such as working as a helper to an experienced mason, or receiving training in the military.

High School Classes

High school is an excellent time to start building your construction skills and knowledge, so that you're well-prepared when it comes time to start an apprenticeship or other training program. In shop classes, you'll learn how to use tools, build basic structures made from bricks and other types of stone, troubleshoot problems as you construct things, and learn many other skills. Some high schools even offer specialized curricula in masonry. For

■ *A young woman learns basic masonry skills via an apprenticeship program.*

example, Shawsheen Valley Technical High School in Massachusetts in the U.S. has a masonry program in which students learn about the following:

31

- Laying brick and block
- Brick and block bonds
- Chimneys, arches, and fireplaces
- Masonry restoration
- Tile setting and stonework
- Ladders and scaffolding
- Workplace safety
- Blueprint reading and estimating
- Building codes
- Applied masonry mathematics, science, and theory.

Masons must know how to add, subtract, multiply, divide, and compute fractions and percentages to calculate various things (such as the number of bricks needed for a certain area, the proper mix of sand and cement, etc.) as they work, so be sure to take math classes, including basic algebra and trigonometry.

If you plan to start your own company, you should take computer science, business, marketing, English/writing, and accounting classes. Taking a foreign language such as Spanish (if you live in the United States) will come in handy if you work in areas where many people do not speak the main language(s) of your country.

Other recommended courses include:

- **Chemistry, geology, and other science classes:** to help you to understand the chemical properties of cement, concrete, mortar, and other substances to ensure that they are mixed and work correctly, as well as to understand the properties and qualities of various types of stone.

- **Blueprint reading:** to learn how to read construction blueprints in order to turn a one-dimensional image on paper or a computer screen into a real, three-dimensional finished product.

- **Physics:** to understand the laws that govern the natural world when building bridges, arches, and other structures.

■ *A college masonry student discusses why she loves the field:*

Pre-Apprenticeships

Some aspiring masons participate in masonry pre-apprenticeship programs before entering an apprenticeship program. This gives them a chance to explore masonry before making a big commitment to an apprenticeship. Such programs are offered by professional associations, community colleges, and unions. In the United States, pre-apprenticeship programs last anywhere from six to twelve weeks. Program lengths vary by country. For example, the masonry pre-apprenticeship program offered by the Ontario Masonry Training Centre in Canada lasts thirty-two to forty weeks.

The International Masonry Training and Education Foundation provides pre-apprenticeship training in the trowel trades: brick, stone, tile, marble, terrazzo, refractory, plaster, cement, and pointing/cleaning/caulking. In this program, you'll learn the basics of stone work (e.g., spreading mortar, laying block and brick to the line, wall types, wall designs, safety practices).

In the United States, Associated Builders and Contractors offers a pre-apprenticeship program that prepares students to enter a registered apprenticeship program. (Registered apprenticeship programs must meet standards of fairness, safety, and training established by the U.S. government or local governments.) Some of the modules completed by participants include:

- Introduction to Construction Math
- Introduction to Hand Tools

33

- Introduction to Power Tools

- Introduction to Construction Drawings

- Introduction to Material Handling

The National Association of Home Builders offers pre-apprenticeship **certificate** training through the Home Builders Institute. The program is geared toward high school and college students, transitioning military members, veterans, justice-involved youth and adults, and unemployed and displaced workers. Programs are available in masonry, plumbing, carpentry, building construction technology, weatherization, electrical, landscaping, and painting.

■ *A stone mason apprentice discusses the rewards of participating in an apprenticeship:*

Apprenticeships

Most masonry workers prepare for the field by completing an apprenticeship program, which, in the United States, typically lasts three to four years, although some programs are shorter. During each year in the program, trainees complete 2,000 hours of on-the-job training and 144 hours of related classroom instruction. Entry requirements vary by program, but typical requirements include:

- Minimum age of eighteen (in Canada and some other countries, the minimum age is sixteen)

- High school education

- One year of high school algebra

■ *Participating in an apprenticeship is a good idea for those who like a structured environment that combines both classroom and hands-on training.*

- Qualifying score on an aptitude test
- Drug free (illegal drugs)

Most apprenticeship training programs combine related instruction with on-the-job training (site preparation, masonry placement and finishing, concrete and mortar repair, decorative masonry, etc.). However, there are other types of training structures. For example, in front-loaded programs, apprentices must complete a certain amount of related instruction before beginning on-the-job training. Segmented apprenticeships require apprentices to alternate between periods of related instruction and on-the-job training.

The International Masonry Training and Education Foundation provides apprenticeship training to the members of the International Union of Bricklayers and Allied Craftworkers. Training is provided at the organization's John J. Flynn BAC/IMI International Training Center in Bowie, Maryland, as well as at local union training centers. The Operative Plasterers' and Cement Masons' International Association (OPCMIA) also offers apprenticeship training. The OPCMIA curriculum covers the following topics:

- Introduction to the industry and trade history
- Identification and proper use of tools

- Material composition and mixes
- Repair and restoration
- Scaffolding and Occupational Safety and Health Administration safety courses
- Blueprint reading
- First-aid and CPR certification

Visit www.doleta.gov/OA/sainformation.cfm for information on apprenticeship training programs in your state.

A typical masonry apprenticeship program in Canada involves three, twelve-month periods. This program includes at least 3,600 hours of on-the-job training, two four-week blocks of technical training, and the completion of a final certificate exam. In Australia, programs last between two and four years.

As they gain experience, apprentices expand their skill sets, take on more responsibility, and earn higher wages. Those who complete a masonry apprenticeship training program are known as *journeymen masons*.

■ *A student (left) learns masonry techniques from an instructor in a community college program.*

36

Masonry Career Path

There are good opportunities for advancement in masonry. Here is a typical career ladder for masonry workers.

Business Owner: Operates a masonry contracting firm that provides services to homeowners and businesses. Typically licensed to offer masonry services.

Project Manager: Oversees masonry work for entire projects. Is responsible for staffing, ordering supplies and equipment, quality control, and other tasks.

Foreman: A journeyman mason who manages a group of other journeymen and apprentices on a project.

Journeyman Mason: Has completed apprenticeship training. If licensed, can work by him- or herself without direct supervision, but, for large projects, must work under permits issued to a masonry contractor.

Apprentice Mason: Apprentice masons complete 2,000 hours of on-the-job training and 144 hours of related classroom instruction during each year of a three- to four-year course of study.

Most U.S. states and some countries require that masonry business owners become licensed; the requirements vary.

Technical and Community College

You can also train to become a mason by earning a certificate, diploma, and/or an associate degree in masonry construction from a technical college or community college. A technical college is a public or private college that offers two- or four-year programs in practical subjects, such as the trades, information technology, applied sciences, agriculture, and engineering. A community college is a private or public two-year school that awards certificates and associate degrees, and sometimes bachelor's degrees. College masonry programs involve both classes and hands-on training via workshops and **internships**. Some of these programs have relationships with formal apprenticeship programs. Typical classes in an associate degree program include:

Which Educational Path is Best for Me?

There are four main ways to prepare to become a mason: apprenticeship, technical/community college, informal training, and military. Let's discuss the pros and cons of each:

Apprenticeship

Pros: The most popular training path for aspiring masonry workers because it provides a clear path to employment. Unlike college, you earn while you learn, and your pay increases as you gain experience. An apprenticeship looks great on your resume (a formal summary of your educational and work experience that is submitted to a potential employer).

Con: Programs typically last three to four to years.

A Good Fit: For those who like a structured environment that combines both classroom and hands-on training.

Technical School/Community College

Pros: Programs are shorter than apprenticeships—typically one to two years.

Cons: You must pay tuition and you do not get paid like apprentices do (unless your program is affiliated with an apprenticeship program).

A Good Fit: For those who want to enter the workforce more quickly.

Informal Training

Pros: Allows you to get to work right away and receive a salary.

Cons: Training might not be as detailed as an apprenticeship or degree program.

A Good Fit: For those who do not need a structured educational setting to learn and who are able to pick up their skills and knowledge on the job.

Military Training

Pros: You receive quality training and a salary, and possibly get to travel the world.

Cons: You'll be required to serve your country for two or more years anyplace in the world, including in a war zone.

A Good Fit: For those who respect authority, can follow instructions, and have a disciplined personality.

- Brick and Block Laying
- Masonry Construction
- Masonry Math
- Tools, Equipment, and Safety
- Advanced Block Laying
- Advanced Brick Laying
- Chimney and Fireplace Construction
- Arch Construction
- Steps, Patios, and Brick Floors
- Foundations

Informal Training Opportunities

You can also train to be a mason by working as a helper to an experienced mason for three to five years. At first, you'll be assigned basic tasks such as setting up work sites and mixing mortar, as you gradually build your skills. If you train this way, it's a good idea to take some college masonry classes or even earn a certificate or diploma to expand your skills and knowledge.

■ *A trainee (left) observes a skilled mason during on-the-job training.*

■ *A U.S. Air Force mason finishes the mortar joints between newly laid bricks in a wall at a school in Honduras.*

Military

The military needs masons to build and repair buildings, bridges, dams, bunkers, and other structures. The U.S. Air Force, Marines, Coast Guard, and Navy, as well as many militaries in other countries, provide training for cement masons and concrete finishers. According to TodaysMilitary.com, training covers topics such as:

- The use of masonry and carpentry tools
- Building construction
- Masonry construction methods
- Types and uses of construction joints and braces
- Interpretation of blueprints and drawings
- How to mix and set concrete, mortar, and plaster
- Cabinetmaking

If you join the military, you don't have to pay for your education, and you get paid for your service. But keep in mind the following as you consider enlisting: you will be required to make a service commitment of several years and you may not receive your first choice for a career. The military decides how it will use your services. So, even if you want to build walls or bridges, you might end up washing dishes in the mess hall or serving on the front lines in a war zone.

Getting a Job

You've completed your training. Now what? You'll either be offered a job as part of your training program, or you'll have to look for a job. Here are some common job-search methods for job seekers. While you won't be looking for a job for a few years, it's a good idea to learn about the job-search process now so that you'll be ready to act when the time comes.

Use Your Network. As a teenager, you may not think you have a network, but you do. Your personal network consists of friends and family. They provide support and information to you as you go about your life. This network might even help you to get your first after-school job at a supermarket or law office. Or if you're taking a high school or college admission exam, people in your network might be able to give you some advice to ace the test.

As you get older and begin training to become a mason, you'll also develop a professional network that consists of the following types of people:

- Fellow apprentices and classmates
- Instructors
- Job superintendents
- People you meet at masonry industry events
- People you meet online, including at social networking sites such as LinkedIn.

You can use this network to learn about job opportunities, talk "shop" with other apprentices or masons, and even apply for a job. The key is to tell as many people as possible that you're looking for a job.

Check Out Job Boards. Job listings can be found on internet job boards that are hosted by government agencies, professional associations, and businesses. At many of these sites, you can search by geographic region, salary, job type, employer name, and other criteria. While you're not ready to look for a job, it will be helpful to read some job listings to see what types of skills and educational backgrounds are in demand. Here are a few popular job boards:

■ *Members of your work team can be good sources of job leads.*

- https://www.linkedin.com
- https://www.usajobs.gov (U.S. government job board)
- https://www.jobbank.gc.ca (Canadian government job board)
- https://www.gov.uk/jobsearch (United Kingdom government job board).

Join and Use the Resources of Unions and Professional Associations. Some masonry workers belong to unions, which are organizations that seek to gain better wages, benefits, and working conditions for their members. They are also called *labor unions* or *trade unions*. The main unions for masonry workers in the United States and Canada are the International Union of Bricklayers and Allied Craftworkers (which is known as the BAC) and the Operative Plasterers' and Cement Masons' International Association. Other unions for masons include UNITE (United Kingdom) and the Building and Allied Trades' Union (Ireland).

There are many benefits to union membership. For example, masons who are members of unions typically receive higher earnings, better benefits (**pension**, health insurance, etc.), and more job security than those who are not members of unions. Additionally, once you are a member of a union, you'll have access to a large network of people who can give you tips on landing a job or even direct you to job openings. Unions, such as the BAC, have job boards where you can look for jobs, and they also offer many training opportunities.

Professional associations are also good resources for aspiring and experienced masons. They offer membership (including categories for students and young workers), training opportunities, networking events, and certification. Most countries have at least one professional association for masonry workers. Here are some major professional associations for masonry workers around the world:

- American Concrete Institute (United States)
- Association of Brickwork Contractors (United Kingdom)
- The Masonry Society (international)
- Mason Contractors Association of America (United States)
- National Bricklayers Association (Australia)
- National Concrete Masonry Association (United States)
- National Guild of Master Craftsmen (Ireland)
- Women in Concrete Alliance (United States)

How Much Can I Earn?

With each passing year, the secret is getting out: a college degree is not the only ticket to a well-paying stable career. Research conducted by government agencies and professional associations shows that skilled trades workers such as masons can earn incomes that are comparable, and sometimes even higher, than those with degrees. And, unlike college students, apprentices begin earning as soon as they begin learning and often don't incur education-related debt. The average U.S. college undergraduate has $37,172 in student loan debt, according to The Institute for College Access & Success. Apprentices typically begin by earning between 40 percent and 50 percent of what trained masons make, and they receive pay increases as they gain experience. And they don't have to pay tuition.

Average Earnings

Average annual salaries for brickmasons and blockmasons are $49,250, according to the U.S. Department of Labor (USDL). Ten percent of brickmasons and block-masons (typically those without much experience) earn $30,070 a year.

The USDL reports the following average annual earnings for brickmasons and block-masons by employer:

Salaries for Brickmasons and Blockmasons by U.S. State

Earnings for brickmasons and blockmasons vary widely by state based on demand and other factors. Here are the five states where employers pay the highest average salary and the states in which employers pay the lowest salaries.

Highest Average Salaries:
1. Massachusetts: $77,540
2. New York: $73,990
3. Illinois: $73,430
4. Washington: $73,180
5. Minnesota: $69,390

Lowest Average Salaries:
1. Mississippi: $35,240
2. Florida: $35,960
3. South Carolina: $36,130
4. Georgia: $36,530
5. North Carolina: $38,050

Source: U.S. Department of Labor

- Residential building construction, $69,210;
- Building finishing contractors, $68,540;
- Local government, $65,410;
- Nonresidential building construction, $62,450;
- Foundation, structure, and building exterior contractors, $51,310;

Cement masons and concrete finishers make less money than brickmasons and blockmasons do. They earn average salaries of $39,180. Earnings range from $26,590 to $68,470 or more.

Helpers to brickmasons, blockmasons, stonemasons, and tile and marble setters earn median salaries of $30,570, according to the USDL. Ten percent of helpers earn less than $21,360, while 10 percent earn $49,990 or more.

Top Earners

The top 10 percent of brickmasons and blockmasons make $84,100 or more, according to the USDL. Who receives this type of pay? The most highly-skilled and experienced workers, those who supervise or manage others, and those who live in large cities and other areas with high demand for masons and a shortage of workers. Masonry contractors with thriving businesses can earn $90,000 to $200,000 or more, depending on the size of their companies.

Union members often receive medical insurance, a pension, and other benefits from their union. Self-employed workers must provide their own fringe benefits.

■ *In the United States, 10 percent of brickmasons and blockmasons make $84,000 or more a year.*

Text-Dependent Questions

1. What high school classes should you take to prepare for training to become a mason?

2. What is the most popular training method for aspiring masons, and how long does this training last?

3. How much can masonry contractors earn?

Research Project

Learn more about apprenticeships by visiting https://www.dol.gov/apprenticeship. Ask your shop teacher or school counselor to help set up an information interview with a masonry apprentice or apprenticeship coordinator to get a better understanding of the apprenticeship process.

ON THE JOB
Interview with a Professional

Robert Arnold is the National Director of Apprenticeship, Training and Educational for the International Masonry Training and Education Foundation. He has been a union bricklayer since 1978.

Q. What made you to get into this field?

A. I got into the trade at the recommendation of my best friend's father who worked at a masonry material yard. I had planned to attend college at Northern Illinois University with an SAT scholarship. My intention was to work through the summer and go to college in the fall. But the money was good, and I enjoyed working outside on buildings that would be around quite a long time, so my career in the masonry field had started. The more I worked in the field, the more I enjoyed what I was doing. I worked on schools, hospitals, apartment buildings, houses, and on industrial jobs and never turned back. After forty years, I still feel the excitement when I step onto a job site and see young individuals enjoy what I enjoy.

Q. Can you provide a brief overview of the typical pre-apprenticeship program for an aspiring masonry worker?

A. A typical apprenticeship program for a union apprentice starts out with what we call a pre-apprenticeship which could last from six to twelve weeks. In this pre-apprenticeship, the student would typically learn the basics of bricklaying. Spreading mortar, laying block and brick to the line, wall types, wall aesthetics, and an understanding of level and plumb are the core of the curriculum. Most importantly, the student would get an understanding of the safety aspects of a masonry job site and, in most cases, have OSHA 10 training before he or she steps onto the job site.

Q. What are the benefits of training via an apprenticeship as opposed to other training methods?

A. Training via an apprenticeship has many advantages; classroom training, related hands-on training, and on-the-job training I would say are the top three. An apprentice is required to attend classes a minimum of 144 hours per year for the duration of the apprenticeship. Most apprenticeships last three or four years. Most of the time on jobsites, no one has time to sit down with an inexperienced employee and teach them the procedures of installing masonry and the many components that are included in a masonry wall system. When an apprentice attends school, the instructor can take his or her time and explain the work process, which is included in the trade curriculum. Although the apprentice spends 95 percent of his/her time on-the-job learning, it is very beneficial to be able to spend time with an experienced masonry instructor to learn all aspects of the trade.

Q. Is there anything that surprises new apprentices about the program?

A. A typical surprise for most apprentices is the pace of the work on a job site. A good journey worker could lay four or five times as many block or brick than a new apprentice and make it look easy.

Q. What kind of personal traits are important for masonry workers?

A. When I have done interviews for potential apprentices in the past, the traits that I look for are first and foremost, did the individual show up on time for the interview? Did he/she follow the directions given for the application process? Did they know anything about the trade through a friend, or had they looked online to see what the trade entails? Most military folks are perfect candidates for our trade—you get up early in the morning, you work safe and hard, and you do it all again tomorrow.

Q. What advice would you give to someone who is considering a career as a masonry professional?

A. The one thing that I tell most people looking for a career in the masonry field is to be persistent. If your heart is set on being a bricklayer, try and if you don't succeed, try again. Many times, an instructor has said to me at the beginning of a pre-apprenticeship, "this guy isn't going to make it," but after a few weeks, most people surprise us. Like most things in life, you must set goals, and set your goals high. I have talked to young apprentices who ask what it takes to be a foreman or how would you go about becoming a contractor. These are goals that take a lot of hard work and perseverance, but are very attainable in our profession.

Q. Will advances in technology ever limit job opportunities for masonry workers?

A. Advances in technology have benefited our trade in one way or another. Mast climbing scaffolding is a perfect example. Instead of working on a frame scaffold in which you may be bending down to your ankles and reaching above your head, mast climbing scaffolds keep the work at waist height which, ergonomically, is much safer and puts less stress on your body. For the last few years we have been working with SAM (the Semi-Automated-Mason). SAM is programmed on the jobsite by a bricklayer who knows how to layout masonry walls, calculate window and door heights, and many other facets of the job. SAM cannot work alone; bricklayers work along with SAM to install things like anchoring systems and insulation. Mortar joints are tooled on one end of the wall while SAM is working on the other. Other technologies such as drones have become a popular tool for mason contractors who do forensic evaluations of older masonry buildings that need repair. Not too long ago, the Washington Monument was damaged by an earthquake. The forensic evaluation was done by scaling down the sides of the monument and taking photos of the damaged area. This can now be done with drones. As technology evolves, masonry workers will always be needed to create the great masonry buildings throughout the country and to repair the iconic structures of the past.

■ *Masons must have good strength and stamina because they often lift heavy stones, bags of mortar and grout, and equipment.*

Words to Understand

ethnic group: A collection of people who have a shared connection based on their homeland, cultural heritage, history, ancestry, language, or other factors.

invoicing: The process of sending a customer a bill for work that has been completed.

nonprofit organization: A group (unlike a corporation or other for-profit business) that uses any profits it generates to advance its stated goals (protecting the environment, helping the homeless, etc.).

resume: A formal summary of your educational and work experience that is submitted to a potential employer.

CHAPTER 5

Key Skills and Methods of Exploration

What All Masonry Workers Need

There's much more to being a good mason than skill with a trowel. Masonry workers need a variety of physical and intellectual characteristics that allow them to be successful on the job, including:

- **Good dexterity, hand speed, and hand–eye coordination.** You will handle bricks, natural stone (marble, granite, limestone, etc.), and other materials frequently as you work, and you must place bricks and stones with precision so that they are aligned correctly. Aligning a few bricks may seem easy, but it quickly becomes a challenge when you have to rapidly and correctly build a massive brick wall or bridge.

■ *Bricklayers must be attentive to detail. Above, a bricklayer uses a level and the handle of his trowel to level bricks.*

49

- **Physical stamina and strength.** You'll need to set a steady pace to stay on schedule. Bricks aren't heavy, but the steady pace of buttering and setting bricks may be tiring. You'll spend a great deal of your day stooping, bending, reaching, and kneeling, as well as climbing ladders or scaffolds. You'll also need to do physically demanding tasks such as splitting block or brick. You may have to carry bags of mortar and grout and equipment that can weigh more than fifty pounds (22.7 kilograms).

- **Unafraid of heights.** You'll occasionally work on scaffolds, ladders, and roofs, so you must not be afraid of heights. You also need good balance and the ability to follow all safety procedures.

- **Artistic ability.** You'll need a good sense of how different colors, patterns, and textures work together to create an attractive finished product.

- **Detail-oriented.** It may seem easy to build a sharp-looking wall or other stone structure, but it is not. Success is in the details. You need to be very attentive to every step in the process. For example, if you fail to mix the mortar correctly, the bricks or other stone will not bond correctly, and your wall will fall. If you don't carefully align the bricks based on the positioning of the mason's line, you'll have an uneven wall face. If you own a masonry business and fail to keep detailed records regarding client **invoicing**, equipment and supplies used, and customer appointments, you won't get paid, will be short of supplies or equipment right when you need them, and will miss customer appointments.

- **Troubleshooting ability.** When repairing a brick wall or other masonry structure, you'll need to use your analytical abilities to identify problems. These range from the obvious (cracked or missing mortar, stains caused by metal corrosion or salts, joints that have not been tooled smooth, etc.) to those that require a little detective work (such as an improperly built foundation under a patio that has caused the sinking or sagging of the bricks). If the mortar is too wet to work with (because of high humidity), the mason may have to remix it to make it drier for current conditions. Additionally, challenges arise during any masonry project (such as the delivery of the wrong type of brick or other building materials, blueprints that do not match what you actually see at the jobsite, unexpected bad weather, etc.) so you'll need to be good at identifying issues and developing creative solutions to solve them.

Did You Know?

The fear of heights is known as acrophobia. Approximately 24 percent of Americans are afraid of heights, according to the Chapman University Survey of American Fears. In Canada, 37 percent of women and 31 percent of men are afraid of heights, according to a survey funded by the Canadian Cancer Society.

- **Teamwork/interpersonal/communication skills.** If you work as a member of a masonry team, you'll need to learn how to work with people from different backgrounds, ethnic groups, ages, and experience levels.

- **Ability to work independently.** You must have a good work ethic, be able to follow instructions, and have a willingness to work hard whether your boss is standing over you observing your work or he or she is ten miles away at another job site.

- **Good color vision.** Terrazzo workers must be able to distinguish between minor variations in color when setting terrazzo patterns to create the most attractive finish. Good color vision is important for any masonry worker because they occasionally need to try to closely match the color of replacement brick and mortar with existing stonework.

- **Business and customer-service skills.** If you're self-employed, you must be friendly with customers, patiently explain the work that needs to be done in terminology they can understand, and be willing to answer their questions. You'll also need be good at marketing your business at community events, in the local newspaper, and on social media; and skilled at bidding on jobs, managing staff, planning payroll, scheduling work appointments, and performing other tasks that keep your company running smoothly.

Exploring Masonry as a Student

There are many ways to learn more about masonry as a middle school or high school student. Classes, clubs, and competitions, do-it-yourself activities, and information interviews are just a few ways to learn more. Here's a rundown of some popular methods of exploration:

■ *Learn how to build a garden wall without mortar:*

Take Some Classes. Several classes will help you to learn more about the construction industry and prepare for a career in masonry. In shop class, for example, you'll learn about construction principles, safety practices, structural blueprint reading, and much more. You'll learn how to use hand and power tools, as well as safety practices. Some schools offer specialized curricula in masonry in their shop classes. In such a program, you'll learn how to use a trowel, level, and other masonry tools; lay brick and block; restore old or damaged masonry; and much more. In some programs, you might build a brick wall or chimney. Other useful classes include math (particularly basic algebra and trigonometry), physics, earth science, chemistry, geology, and, if you plan to start your own company, business, marketing, English/writing, computer science, and accounting classes.

Try Out Some Tools. Masons use many basic tools such as trowels, hammers, levels, and chisels that you might find in your parents' garage, at a hardware store, or at a local library (some have tool lending programs). Your shop teacher and parents can teach you how to use many of these tools. The goal is to become comfortable using these tools, and have fun in the process. Check out YouTube if you're not sure how to use certain tools.

Build Something! Put down that phone, turn off the TV, stop checking Facebook for the umpteenth time, and build a wall, or a mini bridge, or something else with brick or stone. This will give you a chance to learn how to mix mortar, "butter" bricks, carefully align stone, and tackle the design and construction challenges that are part of

■ *A student tries out a hammer and level.*

any building project. These types of projects are also a lot of fun, so get building! Ask your shop teacher to provide project ideas. YouTube is an excellent source of how-to videos. And check out *Black & Decker: The Complete Guide to Concrete & Masonry: Build with Concrete, Brick, Block & Natural Stone* to learn some masonry terminology and get some tips on how to get started.

Join or Start a Construction Club at Your School. Chances are, there are people just like you at your school who are interested in building and repairing things. If so, you should consider starting a masonry or general construction club. Ask your shop teacher to serve as a teacher-advisor for the club. In such a club, you'll learn about construction practices, how to use tools, and how to build things. Your faculty advisor may be able to organize presentations by masons or tours of construction sites. Once your club builds its masonry skills, perhaps the group can volunteer to do minor masonry repairs for the elderly.

Participate in a Competition. Competing in a contest is a good way to make new friends, build your skills, and test your talents against those of your classmates or students from around the country or world. Competitions are sponsored by schools, local park districts, or regional, national, or international membership organizations

53

■ *A masonry student competes in a competition.*

for young people interested in STEM. One such contest was recently held at Buchtel High School in Akron, Ohio. Students from around Ohio and a few from Pennsylvania participated in a masonry contest in which skilled masons judged how plumb, square, and level their work was, as well as the accuracy of their measurements and creativity of their designs. Winners received bragging rights and thousands of dollars' worth of tools and prizes. Here are two well-known organizations that host competitions that will allow you to develop and demonstrate your masonry skills and knowledge:

- **SkillsUSA** (http://www.skillsusa.org) is a "national membership organization serving middle-school, high-school, and college/postsecondary students who are preparing for careers in trade, technical, and skilled service occupations." Its SkillsUSA Championships involve competitions in one hundred events. Students first compete locally, with winners advancing to state and national levels. A small number of winners can even advance to compete against young people from more than seventy-five other countries at WorldSkills International, which was recently held in Abu Dhabi, United Arab Emirates, and in Leipzig, Germany. In the Masonry Competition, students are asked to construct a composite brick and block project that meets industry standards for quality in a six-hour period, as well as pass a written exam. Other competitions are available in Related Technical Math, Architectural Drafting, Engineering Technology/Design, Principles of Engineering/Technology, and other trades. SkillsUSA works directly with high schools and colleges, so ask your school counselor or teacher if it is an option for you.

- **Skills Compétences Canada** (http://skillscompetencescanada.com/en/skills-canada-national-competition). This **nonprofit organization** seeks to encourage Canadian youth to pursue careers in the skilled trades and technology sectors. Its National Competition allows young people to participate in more than forty skilled trade and technology competitions. In the Brick Masonry Competition, competitors must read blueprints to construct brick and block walls or surfaces with brick facing (such as decorative brickwork) and features in a certain amount of time. The work of each competitor is assessed based on the following criteria: dimensions, levelling, plumb, alignment, angles, detail, safety, joint uniformity and finishing, and overall appearance and cleanliness. Other competitions are available in carpentry, sheet metal work, welding, other trades, and workplace safety. In addition to participating in the competitions, student attendees can check out a dedicated "Career Zone" that features exhibitors and participate in Try-A-Trade® and technology activities.

■ *Watch scenes from a recent SkillsUSA Masonry Competition and learn about the strong demand for masons:*

55

■ *During a tour of a construction site, a high school student tries out a level.*

Tour a Construction Site. During a tour, you'll get the chance to see masonry workers on the job. You can ask them what type of stone and building techniques they're using, and you may even get a chance to try out a trowel or learn how to use a mason's line. Ask your school counselor or shop teacher to arrange a tour of a construction site or other place where masons work. Some industry organizations (such as Go Construct in the United Kingdom) arrange tours to educate young people about construction specialties. Local construction associations and unions may also have information on tour opportunities.

Talk to or Job Shadow a Mason. A good way to learn more about this career is to participate in an information interview with a mason. Don't let the "interview" part of "information interview" scare you. This interview does not involve getting your resume in shape or asking for a job, but, instead, you gather information. You'll find that many masons are eager to tell you about their careers. Here are some questions to ask during the interview:

• Can you tell me about a day in your life on the job?

• What's your work environment like? Do you have to travel for your job?

Sources of Additional Exploration

 Contact the following organizations for more information on education and careers in masonry:

American Concrete Institute

http://www.concrete.org

Association of Brickwork Contractors

http://www.associationofbrickworkcontractors.co.uk

International Masonry Institute

http://www.imiweb.org

International Union of Bricklayers and Allied Craftworkers

http://www.bacweb.org

Mason Contractors Association of America

http://www.masoncontractors.org

The Masonry Society

http://www.masonrysociety.org

National Bricklayers Association

https://www.nationalbricklayersassociation.com.au

National Concrete Masonry Association

http://www.ncma.org

National Guild of Master Craftsmen

http://www.nationalguild.ie

National Terrazzo and Mosaic Association

http://www.ntma.com

National Tile Contractors Association

http://www.tile-assn.com

Operative Plasterers' and Cement Masons' International Association

http://www.opcmia.org

Women in Concrete Alliance

http://www.womeninconcretealliance.org

- What are the most challenging tools to use?
- What are the most important personal and professional qualities for people in your career?
- What do you like best and least about your job?
- What do you do to keep yourself safe on the job?
- What is the future employment outlook for masons? How is the field changing?
- What can I do now to prepare for the field?
- What do you think is the best educational path to becoming a mason?

Job shadowing a mason is another way to get a firsthand look at the world of masonry. In this scenario, you follow the mason around for a few hours or even an entire day on the job. You can observe them as they mix mortar, build and repair walls, and perform other duties. You might even get a chance to try out some tools or add a few bricks to a wall.

■ *Volunteering with Habitat for Humanity is a good way to learn more about masonry and help others.*

Unions, professional associations, career counselors, shop teachers, and friends and family who know masons can help you arrange an information interview or job shadowing experience.

Volunteer and Learn. Consider volunteering with a local or other community group that builds or repairs homes. This will give you a chance to watch skilled masons and other construction professionals at work, and do some good. One organization to investigate is Habitat for Humanity, which operates in nearly 1,400 communities across the U.S. and in more than seventy countries around the world to build affordable housing and repair existing homes for those in need. Through its Youth Programs (https://www.habitat.org/volunteer/near-you/youth-programs), Habitat for Humanity offers volunteer opportunities for those age five to forty. High school and college students can start a Habitat chapter at their schools, volunteer to build or fix houses for a week during school breaks, and get involved in other activities that allow them to learn about home construction and make the world a better place.

 Text-Dependent Questions

1. Why is it important for a masonry worker to be good at troubleshooting?

2. What is SkillsUSA and what does it offer to students?

3. What is an information interview? What questions should you ask during such an interview?

 Research Project

Masonry workers must be in good physical shape to be successful on the job. Learn more about how to stay fit and healthy by visiting https://www.healthychildren.org/English/ages-stages/teen/fitness/Pages/How-Teens-Can-Stay-Fit.aspx, http://www.safeteens.org/nutrition-exercise/exercise-fitness, and https://www.hhs.gov/fitness/be-active/ways-to-be-active/index.html. Set daily health and fitness goals for yourself and keep a record of your progress.

■ *A construction mason lays bricks. Employment for masons in the commercial construction industry is expected to be strong in the next decade.*

Words to Understand

Baby Boomer: A person who was born from the early-to-mid 1940s through 1964.

radio waves: Electronic signals that are generated by a transmitter and then detected by a receiver.

recession: A period of economic decline in one country, several countries, or worldwide, in which many banks fail, the real estate sector crashes, trade declines, and many people lose their jobs.

sustainability: In the construction industry, an emphasis on building practices that save energy or reduce energy output, that use building materials from renewable resources such as wood and stone that can also be recycled or reused, and that incorporate other environmentally-friendly practices.

CHAPTER 6

The Future of the Mason Occupation

The Big Picture

Brick is an extremely popular building material because of its durability, attractiveness, fire-resistance, and sustainability. Other masonry materials—concrete, natural-cut stone, and terrazzo—also remain popular. As a result, demand should continue to be strong for masonry workers to build and repair walls, bridges, dams, floors, and other structures. But despite strong demand, there's a shortage of skilled workers in many countries. One main reason for this shortage is that many Baby Boomers are retiring from the trades, and not enough young people are entering the field to replace them. Many young people have come to accept myths about masonry careers—that they are too physically demanding and dirty, that they are only for people who couldn't make it in college, and that they do not pay well. Construction educators and associations are busting these stereotypes. They point out that masons certainly get dirty on the job, but they also use their brain power to solve problems. New technologies have also been developed that

■ *Demand is expected to be strong for masonry workers in Australia.*

61

reduce the physical demands on masons. Finally, brickmasons in the United States earn average salaries of $53,440, according to the U.S. Department of Labor (USDL). This salary is higher than the average earnings ($49,630) for all workers. Masons who become managers or who launch their own businesses can have earnings that range from $90,000 to $200,000. These facts are nothing to shake a trowel at.

But let's go back to the employment picture. There is a worldwide shortage of masons and other skilled trades workers, according to the human resource consulting firm ManpowerGroup. Globally, workers in the skilled trades were cited by employers as the most in-demand occupational field. By continent/region, skilled trades workers topped the most in-demand list in the Americas, Europe, the Middle East, and Africa.

■ *Employment for masonry workers is expected to grow as many older masons retire in the next decade.*

62

They ranked fourth in the Asia-Pacific region. The top reasons globally that employers can't find talent are lack of available applicants, lack of technical skill, and lack of experience.

The recruitment firm Michael Page recently conducted research to determine demand for specific careers by country. It found that there is a shortage of stonemasons in Germany, Switzerland, Sweden, and Australia.

There are also strong employment opportunities for masonry workers in the United States. Employment for masonry workers is expected to grow anywhere from 10 percent (stonemasons) to 13 percent (concrete masons and finishers) during the next decade, according to the U.S. Department of Labor. This is faster than the average growth (7 percent) expected for all occupations. There will be many new jobs for masons because of the following factors:

- Many masons are reaching retirement age and there are not enough young people entering the field to replace them.

- The number of commercial, public, and civil construction projects (new buildings, bridges, roads) is increasing.

- Population growth is creating a residential building boom, and masons will be needed to construct buildings, schools, and other structures.

- Masons will be needed to repair or replace walls and other structures after hurricanes, tornadoes, earthquakes, and other natural disasters.

■ *A female bricklayer discusses the rewards and challenges of working in the field:*

63

Women in Masonry

Women make up 47 percent of the U.S. workforce, but only 1 percent of masons are female. This percentage is much too low, and industry leaders and associations are trying to increase the number of women entering this exciting and rewarding field. Here are a few organizations that exist to support women in masonry and the construction industry:

- The **Women in Concrete Alliance** offers mentoring, industry events, and other opportunities for women working in the concrete construction industry.
  See http://www.womeninconcretealliance.org.

- The **National Association of Women in Construction** (NAWIC, http//www.nawic.org) offers membership, an annual meeting, and scholarships. It also publishes *The NAWIC IMAGE*.

- The **Canadian Association of Women in Construction** (http://www.cawic.ca) offers membership, a mentoring program, networking events, and a job bank at its website.

New Technologies

For years, not much changed in the world of masons. They continued to use trowels, chisels, hammers, and mortar just like masons had done for thousands of years. But, in recent years, technology has begun to alter the way masons train for and do their jobs.

Apprenticeship programs now incorporate computer simulations and smart boards to help apprentices learn masonry concepts. Masonry contractors use building information modeling software, a computer application that incorporates a 3D model-based process to more efficiently plan, design, and construct buildings and their masonry components. On the job, masons review blueprints and diagrams on tablet computers, and they use laser levels, thermal imaging scanners, and other technology to do their jobs more efficiently.

■ *Masonry associations and unions are trying to encourage more women to enter this exciting field.*

Above job sites, drones whiz through the air, serving as the eyes of masons in hard-to-reach or dangerous areas. The drones reduce the amount of time needed to inspect existing or new masonry. Some contractors now use drones to capture images of a large worksite that could only be taken via a costlier helicopter flyby in the past. Others are using drones to monitor workers and to identify safety issues on site. One caveat: drones can be damaged by high winds and heavy rain. Their performance can also be negatively affected by interference from **radio waves**.

■ *A mason operates a drone at a construction site.*

66

Masonry contractors use office and customer management software to create estimates and invoices, schedule appointments, maintain inventories of supplies and equipment, and for other tasks. They also use the internet and social media to market their businesses and communicate with customers and coworkers.

Mast climbing work platforms, also known as mast climbers, are increasingly being used in place of traditional scaffolds at construction sites. "Mast climbers have a power-driven work platform that climbs a vertical tower, allowing them to reach much higher and carry greater loads than traditional scaffolds," according to the CPWR Work Group on Mast Climbing Work Platforms. "Mast climbers offer many advantages over other forms of scaffolding. They are quicker to erect and dismantle, and they are potentially much better at reducing the risk of shoulder and lower back injuries to workers, since they can be adjusted to an optimum working height."

Masonry software, new tools, drones, and other technology have certainly changed the way in which masons do their jobs, but one recent development promises to significantly change life for masons in coming years. Meet SAM (an acronym for Semi-Automated-Mason), a bricklaying robot. SAM was created by a company named Construction Robotics in 2015, and it is now working at job sites across the world. SAM can lay about eight hundred to twelve hundred bricks a day—as compared to the three hundred to five hundred bricks that a human mason can lay in the same amount of time. SAM works in cooperation with a human mason. The human handles the more nuanced tasks: setting up the worksite, programming SAM with the specifics of the job in question, selecting and loading only quality bricks (SAM is unable to identify flawed bricks), loading mortar,

67

cleaning up excess mortar, laying bricks in tight areas such as corners, striking joints, installing insulation, waterproofing and caulking, and assuring overall quality. SAM picks up the bricks, applies mortar, and places them in the appropriate spot. It is best used at sites with long swaths of flat walls, such as those found at the construction sites of hospitals, universities, and other large buildings. As it exists now, SAM is a complement to human masons, saving companies time and reducing the physical demands of the job. One major concern is that future, improved versions of SAM may significantly reduce the number of masons needed on a job. But since this technology is so new, it is too early to gauge its effects on the mason workforce.

Change has come to the masonry industry, and steady advances in technology suggest that this is just the beginning. Masons who stay up-to-date with technology will have better job prospects than those who do not do so.

■ *Watch SAM, the bricklaying robot, at work:*

Challenges to Employment Growth

It's a great time to be a masonry worker, but it's important to be aware of trends that may slow employment growth. Advances in technology (such as SAM, the bricklaying robot) may reduce the number of masons who are needed. But this technology is expensive and cannot be used for every type of project, so there will still be a need for masons. Additionally, bricklaying robots still must work in cooperation with flesh-and-blood bricklayers, so demand will continue. There will also be a need for masons to identify and fix issues with masonry—something that a robot is not yet able to do.

If another recession occurs, government funding for new construction projects will evaporate, and the public will have less money to spend on masonry repairs or new masonry projects. As a result, fewer masons will be needed.

Finally, skilled masons are in short supply around the world, but if a lot of people decide to enter the field, the number of job opportunities will decline. But this is only a potential future, and current demand for masonry workers is strong.

■ Learn how drones are being used in the masonry industry:

Did You Know?

- About 292,500 masonry workers are employed in the United States. Cement masons and concrete finishers make up 61 percent of this group; brickmasons and blockmasons, 31 percent; stonemasons, 7 percent; and terrazzo workers and finishers, less than 1 percent.

- Approximately 30 percent of bricklayers are self-employed. Only 2.4 percent of cement masons and concrete finishers work for themselves.

- About 9 percent of workers in the construction industry are women.

Source: U.S. Department of Labor

In Closing

Is a career as a mason a good fit for you? If you like turning a pile of bricks into a beautiful building, enjoy working both with your hands and mind, and like the fact that no day on the job is the same as another, the answer is yes. And the good pay (top earners in the U.S. make $90,000 or more annually) and strong employment prospects worldwide make this career a rock-solid option for those who don't want to pursue a four-year degree. I hope that you'll use this book as a starting point to discover even more about a career as a mason. Talk to masons about their careers and shadow them on the job, use the resources of professional organizations, and try building a mini-brick wall or other stone structure at home to learn more about the field. Good luck on your career exploration!

■ *Opportunities for masonry workers are available throughout the world. Above, a mason cuts marble.*

Text-Dependent Questions

1. Why is employment strong for masonry workers?

2. How has technology changed the work of masons?

3. What are some developments that might slow employment for masons?

Research Project

Learn more about the major new technologies—drones, mast climbing work platforms, SAM, etc.—in the masonry sector. Write a report that summarizes your findings.

Series Glossary of Key Terms

apprentice: A trainee who is enrolled in a program that prepares them to work as a skilled trades worker. Apprentices must complete 2,000 hours of on-the-job training and 144 hours of related classroom instruction during a four- to five-year course of study. They are paid a salary that increases as they obtain experience.

apprenticeship: A formal training program that often consists of 2,000 hours of on-the-job training and 144 hours of related classroom instruction per year for four to five years.

bid: A formal offer created by a contractor or trades worker that details the work that will be done, the amount the company or individual will charge, and the time frame in which the work will be completed.

blueprints: A reproduction of a technical plan for the construction of a home or other structure. Blueprints are created by licensed architects.

building codes: A series of rules established by local, state, regional, and national governments that ensure safe construction. The National Electrical Code, which was developed by the National Fire Protection Association, is an example of a building code in the United States.

building information modeling software: A computer application that uses a 3D model-based process that helps construction, architecture, and engineering professionals to more efficiently plan, design, build, and manage buildings and infrastructure.

building materials: Any naturally-occurring (clay, rocks, sand, wood, etc.) or human-made substances (steel, cement, etc.) that are used to construct buildings and other structures.

building permit: Written permission from a government entity that allows trades workers to construct, alter, or otherwise work at a construction site.

community college: A private or public two-year college that awards certificates and associate degrees.

general contractor: A licensed individual or company that accepts primary responsibility for work done at a construction site or in another setting.

72

green construction: The planning, design, construction, and operation of structures in an environmentally responsible manner. Green construction stresses energy and water efficiency, the use of eco-friendly construction materials (when possible), indoor environmental quality, and the structure's overall effects on its site or the larger community. Also known as **green building**.

inspection: The process of reviewing/examining ongoing or recently completed construction work to ensure that it has been completed per the applicable building codes. Construction and building inspectors are employed by government agencies and private companies that provide inspection services to potential purchasers of new construction or remodeled buildings.

job foreman: A journeyman (male or female) who manages a group of other journeymen and apprentices on a project.

journeyman: A trades worker who has completed an apprenticeship training. If licensed, he or she can work without direct supervision, but, for large projects, must work under permits issued to a master electrician.

Leadership in Energy and Environmental Design (LEED) certification: A third-party verification that remodeled or newly constructed buildings have met the highest criteria for water efficiency, energy efficiency, the use of eco-friendly materials and building practices, indoor environmental quality, and other criteria. LEED certification is the most popular green building rating system in the world.

master trades worker: A trades professional who has a minimum level of experience (usually at least three to four years as a licensed professional) and who has passed an examination. Master trades workers manage journeymen, trades workers, and apprentices.

prefabricated: The manufacture or fabrication of certain components of a structure (walls, electrical components, etc.) away from the construction site. Prefabricated products are brought to the construction site and joined with existing structures or components.

schematic diagram: An illustration of the components of a system that uses abstract, graphic symbols instead of realistic pictures or illustrations.

self-employment: Working for oneself as a small business owner, rather than for a corporation or other employer. Self-employed people are responsible for generating their own income, and they must provide their own fringe benefits (such as health insurance).

73

smart home technology: A system of interconnected devices that perform certain actions to save energy, time, and money.

technical college: A public or private college that offers two- or four-year programs in practical subjects, such as the trades, information technology, applied sciences, agriculture, and engineering.

union: An organization that seeks to gain better wages, benefits, and working conditions for its members. Also called a **labor union** or **trade union**.

zoning permit: A document issued by a government body that stipulates that the project in question meets existing zoning rules for a geographic area.

zoning rules: Restrictions established by government bodies as to what type of structure can be built in a certain area. For example, many cities have zoning rules that restrict the construction of factories in residential areas.

Index

Photo Credits

Further Reading & Internet Resources

Addis, Bill. *Building: 3,000 Years of Design, Engineering, and Construction*. New York: Phaidon Press, 2015.

Dykstra, Alison. *Green Construction: An Introduction to a Changing Industry*. San Francisco: Kirshner Books, 2016.

Editors of Cool Springs Press. *Black & Decker: The Complete Guide to Concrete & Masonry: Build with Concrete, Brick, Block & Natural Stone*. 4th ed. Minneapolis, Minn.: Cool Springs Press, 2015.

Kreh, Richard T. *Masonry Skills*. 7th ed. Boston, Mass.: Delmar Cengage Learning, 2014.

Internet Resources

http://www.masonryforlife.com: This website from the Arizona Masonry Guild provides information on the benefits of masonry, answers to frequently asked questions about masonry, an overview of the tools and materials used in masonry, and information on education and careers.

https://www.bls.gov/ooh/construction-and-extraction/brickmasons-block-masons-and-stonemasons.htm#tab-1: This article from the *Occupational Outlook Handbook* provides information on job duties, educational requirements, salaries, and the employment outlook for masonry workers.

http://www.byf.org: This web initiative of the National Center for Construction Education and Research offers overviews of more than thirty careers in the trades, videos of trades workers on the job, and much more.

http://www.careersinconstruction.ca/en/careers/career-finder: This website from BuildForce Canada provides information on job duties, training, and salaries for bricklayers and concrete finishers. It also features interesting videos depicting what it's like to be a bricklayer.

https://nationalcareersservice.direct.gov.uk/job-profiles: This resource from the United Kingdom's National Careers Service provides information on job duties, educational requirements, key skills, salaries, and the work environment for bricklayers and stonemasons.

About the Author

Andrew Morkes has been a writer and editor for more than 25 years. He is the author of more than 20 books about college-planning and careers, including many titles in this series, the *Vault Career Guide to Social Media*, and *They Teach That in College!?: A Resource Guide to More Than 100 Interesting College Majors*, which was selected as one of the best books of the year by the library journal *Voice of Youth Advocates*. He is also the author and publisher of "The Morkes Report: College and Career Planning Trends" blog.

Video Credits

Chapter 1: Check out the top ten reasons to become a bricklayer: http://x-qr.net/1DAo

Learn more about a career as a union cement mason: http://x-qr.net/1Eix

Chapter 4: A college masonry student discusses why she loves the field: http://x-qr.net/1Ggw

A stone mason apprentice discusses the rewards of participating in an apprenticeship: http://x-qr.net/1Gmw

Chapter 5: Learn how to build a garden wall without mortar: http://x-qr.net/1Gb2

Watch scenes from a recent SkillsUSA Masonry Competition and learn about the strong demand for masons: http://x-qr.net/1H5o

Chapter 6: A female bricklayer discusses the rewards and challenges of working in the field: http://x-qr.net/1Goe

Watch SAM, the bricklaying robot, at work: http://x-qr.net/1Dqb

Learn how drones are being used in the masonry industry: http://x-qr.net/1HVh